A LITTLE TREASURY OF
LIMERICKS
FAIR AND FOUL

A LITTLE TREASURY OF LIMERICKS FAIR AND FOUL

JOHN LETTS

Illustrated by Ralph Steadman

A PAN ORIGINAL

PAN BOOKS LTD
LONDON AND SYDNEY

First published 1973 by Pan Books Ltd,
Cavaye Place, London SW10 9PG
ISBN 0 330 23666 0
2nd Printing 1975
This Collection © John Letts 1973
Illustrations © Ralph Steadman 1973

Printed in Great Britain by
Richard Clay (The Chaucer Press) Ltd, Bungay, Suffolk

Contents

Acknowledgements

The following are to be thanked for their contributions, resulting from newspaper advertisements: D. C. Manison, Esq; Miss Diana Clarke; Geoffrey Payton, Esq; G. J. Blundell, Esq; Mrs M. Reed; J. A. Lindon, Esq; J. Wallace, Esq; Duncan Fallowell, Esq; Fred Heneglan, Esq; and John Holbrook, Esq.

There was a young lady called Gloria
Who was had by a Major Pretoria.
She was had by more men
And then had again
By the Band of the Waldorf Astoria

RALPH STEADMAN

Introduction

This new collection contains some three hundred limericks, over a hundred of them hitherto unpublished. That in itself is the best reason for producing another anthology to add to those previously published. The corpus of repeatable limericks needs to be reviewed periodically, and I expect that limerick anthologies will still be appearing from time to time in the next century.

To achieve a healthy renewal, advertisements were placed in *Punch* (traditionally a happy hunting ground for limerick writers), in *Private Eye*, in *The Spectator*, and the personal column of *The Times*. The last paper gracefully but firmly refused to print the text taken by others, which included the following verse:

> There once was a Curate from Kew
> Who preached with his vestments askew:
> A lady called Morgan
> Caught sight of the organ,
> And promptly passed out in the pew.

At that point I considered, but rejected, the idea of running an additional competition for Limericks Suitable for *The Times* to Print.

For whatever reason, the standard of entries was low, and in the event only ten survived to be printed here.

From seventy-odd entries this was disappointing. Easily the best set came from Geoffrey Payton, five of whose verses are among the ten. Of the remainder, some came from friends who wish to remain anonymous (in Sotheby's catalogues they would be described as 'The property of a gentleman'), and many others were acquired by or written by me.

As to the criteria of selection, one can hardly do better than quote the most elegant and witty of the dozen or so limericks about The Limerick so far recorded:

> The limerick packs laughs anatomical
> Into space that is quite economical.
>> But the good ones I've seen
>> So seldom are clean,
> And the clean ones so seldom are comical.

An excellent thought to bear in mind, and I have tried to apply the implied test to every entry in this book. Like other editors before me, I will also try to provide some answers to that insoluble question – exactly what is the enduring attraction of this superficially restrictive and trivial verse form? Part of the answer, I think, is that it has always proved a beautifully simultaneous way of shocking people or notions worth shocking, and at the same time amusing a different set of people worth amusing. I like limericks that are technically perfect in metre. I like limericks with a fifth line so neat and conclusive that one feels one has been struck. I like limericks that have a dotty logic of their own. I like limericks that make a triumphant success of rhyming the un-rhymable in true Ogden Nash tradition. I don't mind limericks being rude, provided they are funny with it.

For these reasons, for all its size and daemonic energy, I find it difficult to read the largest collection of recent years, *The Limerick* (published in Paris in 1953) except as a duty. The four best collections are Langford Reed (1925), Norman Douglas' *Some Limericks* (1928), Louis Untermeyer's 1961 collection and, perhaps best of all, W. S. Baring-Gould's *The Lure of the Limerick* (1968). My grateful thanks go to these predecessors, and I think the last two will realize that it would be impossible to make a good collection without including much that has appeared in their pages. If there is a difference of emphasis, I suspect it may arise from the fact that the oral tradition recorded in their works is American, despite the fact that the bulk of the output has been English. At all events, this seems to be about the first mainly English collection since Langford Reed.

London, December 1972

PS – A birthday card to the editor from his youngest son . . .

There once was a man called McKoo
Whose hobby was squatting on the loo.
He didn't mind sitting all day:
Sometimes he got so tired, instead of sitting, he lay . . .
When he married his wife, she sat there too.

The English Vice

According to some continentals, the English Vice is flogging. But foreigners often have distorted views on these matters (the Italians, for instance, refer to that excellent English pudding 'trifle' as 'Zuppa Inglese'). For my part, I think perverse spelling has a much better claim to the title of the official English Vice than flogging, flagellation or anything else. Happily, it is a vice that has frequently been mocked in limericks – indeed in some of the cleanest and the funniest ever written. Some of these admittedly appear under other headings. But there are sufficient left over to require a section of their own. They were an early development in the history of the limerick; many of the best emerging in the Punch competitions in the late Victorian era.

> There was a young lady of Slough
> Who said that she didn't know hough.
> Then a young fellow caught her
> And jolly well taught her:
> And she can't have enough of it nough.

> There was a young lass from Helvellyn
> Who eloped with the Vicar of Welwyn.
> But the local hotelwyn
> The rear had a wellwyn:
> And they never got wed, for they fellwyn.

There was a young curate of Salisbury*
Whose manners were Halisbury-Scalisbury,
He wandered round Hampshire
Without any pampshire
Till the Vicar compelled him to Walisbury.
*or Sarum

There once was a Duchess of Belvoir*
Who slept with her golden retrelvoir.
Said the choleric Duke:
'These girls make me puke –
And but for the dog I would lelvoir.'
*Or Beever

There was a young fellow called Fisher
Who was fishing for fish in a fissure.
Then a cod with a grin
Pulled the fisherman in . . .
Now they're fishing the fissure for Fisher.

A young Irish servant in Drogheda
Had a mistress who often annogheda,
Whereon she would swear
In a language so rare
That thereafter no one emplogheda.

There was a young fellow of Beaulieu
Who loved a fair maiden most treaulieu.
Said he 'Wilt thou be mine?'
When she didn't decline
The wedding was solemnized deaulieu.

There was a young fellow from Gloucester
Whose wife ran away with a coucester.
He traced her to Leicester
And tried to arreicester –
But in spite of his efforts, he loucester.

She turned up soon after in Bicester
Where the coucester was seen to have kicester.
He caught her at Worcester
Where roundly he gorcester –
And finally married her sicester.

There was a young cashier of Calais
Whose accounts when reviewed wouldn't talais.
But his chief smelled a rat
When he furnished a flat
And was seen every night at the Balais.

A pretty young teacher named Beauchamp
Said, 'These awful boys! How shall I teauchamp?
I try to look grave
But they *will* not behave
– Though with tears in my eyes I besauchamp.'

In New Orleans dwelled a young Creole
Who, when asked if her hair was all reole,
Replied with a shrug,
'Just give it a tug
And decide by the way that I squeole.'

There was a young lady of Twickenham
Whose shoes were too tight to walk quickenham.
She came back from a walk
Looking whiter than chalk
And took them both off and was sickenham.

There was a young lady called Wemyss
Who, it seems, was afflicted with dremyss.
She would wake in the night
And in terrible fright,
Shake the beams of the house with her scremyss.

There once was a choleric colonel
Who used oaths both obscene and infolonel,
Till the Chaplain, aghast,
Gave up protest at last
And just wrote them down in his jolonel.

There was a young lady of Glamis
Who would undress without any qualmis.
She would strip to the buff
For enough of the stuff
And freely dispose of her chalmis.

In her bed, a girl in St Thomas
Once found a strange pair of pajhomas.
Said the girl, 'Well well well!
Whose they are I can't tell –
Something tells me those garments St Mhomas.'

There was once an eccentric Strine*
Whose speech was so sesquipedine,
And his vowels so refined
That their patience got strined,
And they treated him just like an ine.
*Or Australian

Said a Sassenach back in Dun Laoghaire
'I pay homage to nationalist thaoghaire,
But wherever I drobh
I found signposts that strobh
To make touring in Ireland so draoghaire.'

There was a young chappie named Cholmondeley
Who always at dinner sat dolmondeley.
His fair partner said
As he crumbled his bread:
'Dear me! You behave very rolmondeley.'

Said a pretty young mammy in Padua
To her master, 'Please sir, you're a dadua.
I've come for some pins
For to wrap up the twins,
And to hear you remark, sir, how gladua.'

A charming young lady named Geoghegan
(Whose Christian names are less peoghegan),
Will be Mrs Knollys
Very soon at All Ksollys,
But the date is at present a veoghegan.

There was a mechanic of Alnwick
Whose feelings were anti-germanwick.
So when war had begun
He constructed a gun
Whose dimensions were simply titanwick.

There was a young lady of Lancashire,
Who once went to work as a bank cashier.
But she scarcely knew
One plus one equalled two
So they had to revert to a man cashier.

Said a man to his wife in East Sydenham;
'My best trousers! Now where have you hydenham?
It is perfectly true
They were not very new
But I foolishly left half a quidenham.'

There was a young girl from Bayeux
Whose hemlines got hayeux and hayeux.
But the size of her thighs
Provoked only surprise
And extinguished the flames of desayeux.

There was a young lady from Leicester
Who allowed her young men to moleicester.
When they shouted abuse
She would take off her shoes:
But she took off much more when they preicester.

There was an old man of the Isles
Who suffered severely from pisles.
He couldn't sit down
Without a deep frown,
So he had to row standing for misles.

'I wouldn't be bothered with drawers'
Says one of our better-known whawers
'There isn't much doubt
I do better without
In handling my everyday chawers.'

Now what in the hell shall we dioux
With the bloody and murderous Sioux,
Who some time ago
Took up arrow and bow,
And made such a hullabalioux?

There was a young Spaniard from Sitges
Who kept all the tourists in stitges
By parading around
With an ominous frown
And a banana in front of his britges.

A man hired by John Smith & Co.
Loudly declared he would tho.
Man that he saw
Dumping dirt near his store.
The drivers, therefore, didn't do.

She frowned and called him Mr.
Because he boldly kr.
And so in spite
That very night
This Mr. Kr. Sr.

When you think of the hosts without No.
Who are slain by the deadly cuco.
Its quite a mistake
Of such food to partake:
It results in a permanent slo.

Said the specialist in Psychty.
My treatment of course is Pty.
And to cure you I fear
Will take nearly 1 yr.
It's got to be done in enty.

Evangeline Alice Du Bois
Committed a dreadful faux pas.
She loosened a stay
In her decolleté
Exposing her je ne sais quoi.

Of the Georges, it's thought that the Ist
Although bad, was by no means the worst.
The IIIrd one is reckoned
Much worse than the second,
And the IInd much worse than the first.

There was a young fellow from Diss
Who asked his friend's wife for a kiss.
Said the young lady, 'Thrs.
All wrong for a Mrs.
When a Mrs. no longer a Miss.'

Her husband was forced to assistr.
In restraining the lecherous Mr.
Said he, 'Please desist –
She dislikes being kissed –
You'll have to make do with her Sr.'

For years all the young men had struthven
To seduce a young lady called Ruthven,
Once a plumber called Bert
Got his hand up her skirt –
And his plumbing was never forguthven.

The Horrible Double Ontong

Not much less of an English Vice – certainly in the Limerick – is what is best classed as 'the horrible double ontong'. It has a long and respectable ancestry, and again includes some good clean verse. What better to start with than the original:

> There was a young man of Hong Kong
> Who invented a topical song.
> It wasn't the words
> That bothered the birds
> But the horrible double ontong.

> There was a young fellow called Hyde
> Who fell down a privy and died.
> His unfortunate brother
> Then fell down another
> And now they're interred side by side.

> There was a young fellow called Willie
> Whose behaviour was frequently silly.
> At a big UNO ball,
> Dressed in nothing at all,
> He claimed that his costume was Chile.

A publisher went off to France
In search of a tale of romance.
A Parisian lady
Told a story so shady
That the publisher made an advance.

There once was a barber called Hone,
A young man of considerable tone,
He would tell you when drunk:
'I smell like a skunk,'
– But the odour was Eau de Cologne.

There was an old fellow from Eire
Who perpetually sat on the fire.
When they asked 'Are you hot?'
He declared 'I am not –
I am Pat Winterbottom Esquire.'

There was a young girl with a hernia
Who said to her doctor 'Goldernia –
When improving my middle
Be sure you don't fiddle
With matters that do not concernia.'

There once were some learned MDs
Who captured some germs of disease,
And infected a train,
Which, without causing pain,
Allowed hundreds to catch it with ease.

There was a young fellow named Hall
Who fell in the spring in the fall.
'Twould have been a sad thing
Had he died in the spring,
But he didn't, he died in the fall.

There was a young lady called Banker
Who slept while her ship lay at anchor.
She awoke in dismay
When she heard some men say
'Hi! Hoist up the top sheet and spank her.'

There was a young girl, a sweet lamb,
Who smiled as she entered a tram.
And as she embarked
The conductor remarked:
'Your fare.' And she said 'Yes, I am.'

Other fine examples of the genre depend on the extreme
ingenuity of the rhyming, as in the following examples:

There was an eccentric old boffin
Who remarked, in a fine fit of coughing:
'It isn't the cough
That carries you off:
It's the coffin they carry you off in.'

There once was a sinister Ottoman:
To the fair sex, I fear, he was not a man.
He evaded the charms
Of feminine arms:
'Quite frankly,' he said, 'I'm a bottom man.'

There was a young fellow called Lancelot
Whom his neighbours all looked on askance a lot.
Whenever he'd pass
A presentable lass
The front of his pants would advance a lot.

A fellow with passions quite gingery
Was exploring his young sister's lingerie:
When with evident pleasure
He plundered her treasure –
Adding incest to insult and injury.

Two beauties who dwelt by the Bosphorous
Had eyes that were brighter than phosphorous.
The Sultan called, 'Troth!
I'll marry you both!'
But they laughed: 'I'm afraid you must tossphorous.'

There was a young man at the War Office
Whose brain was no good as a store office.
Every warning severe
Just went in at one ear
And out at the opposite orifice.

A lady there was in Antigua
Who said to her spouse 'What a pigua.'
He answered 'My queen
Is it manners you mean –
Or do you refer to my figua?'

There was a young fellow named Sydney
Who drank till he ruined his kidney.
It shrivelled and shrank
As he sat there and drank,
But he had a good time at it, didn't he?

From the Bench said the senile Judge Percival,
'Young man, Counsel claims you'll get worse if I'll
Send you to jail
So I'll put you on bail.'
Now wasn't Judge Percival merciful?

A handsome young bastard named Ray
Was conceived on the Rue de la Paix.
According to law
He can name you his ma:
But as for his pa, je ne sais.

The girls who frequent picture palaces
Set no store by psychoanalysis.
Indeed, they're annoyed
By the great Dr Freud,
And they cling to their long-standing fallacies.

There was a young man from Natal:
And Sue was the name of his gal.
He went off one day
A rather long way
– In fact, right up Suez Canal.

An eccentric old spinster called Lowell
Announced to her friends 'Bless my sowell –
I've gained so much weight
I am sorry to state
I fear that I'm going to fowell'.

Said the Boy King: 'I fear I've a funny
Feeling down here in my tummy.'
'Tut, tut!' said old Ra
I can see that you are
Not a Son, nor a Dad, but a Mummy.'

A colonel called out with great force
In the midst of Hyde Park for a horse.
All the soldiers looked round –
But none could be found:
So he just rhododendron. Of course.

There once was a belle from Toulon
Who said to her beau, 'Pas si bon!
I admire your technique
It's really tres chic . . .
But you're still both Toulouse and Toulon.'

A man in a bus queue at Stoke
Unzipped all his flies for a joke.
An old man gave a shout
And almost passed out –
And a lady close by had a stroke.

An innocent lady in Cicester
One day asked an elderly visitor:
'Now why's it illicit
For a girl to solicit –
When a man can become a solicitor?'

A Classical man from Victoria,
In a post-alcoholic euphoria,
Was discovered one day
In a club for the gay –
Immersed in an Ars Amatoria.

One Longbottom, climbing Ben Nevis
Fell forty feet into a crevice.
He was wedged by Ars Longa –
Recovered – got stronger –
Then passed out – RIP – Vita Brevis.

A dentist named Archibald Moss
Fell in love with the dainty Miss Ross.
Since he held in abhorrence
Her Christian name, Florence,
He renamed her his dear dental floss.

A Sort of Zoo

This is a category rarely dealt with separately by previous anthologists – perhaps because sex has had an understandable tendency to steal its thunder.

Two absolutely classic rhymes to begin:

> There was a young lady of Riga
> Who smiled as she rode on a tiger;
> They returned from the ride
> With the lady inside
> And the smile on the face of the tiger.

> A wonderful bird is the pelican
> His bill can hold more than his bellican.
> He can take in his beak
> Enough food for a week
> I'm damned if I know how the hell he can!

Here are some others to join the menagerie:

> If you wish to descend from a camel,
> That oddly superior mammal,
> You just have to jump
> From the hump on his rump:
> He won't just stop dead like a tram'll.

Consider the poor hippopotamus:
His life is unduly monotonous.
He lives half asleep
At the edge of the deep –
And his face is as big as his bottom is.

You'd require an extremely long scarf
If you happened to be a giraffe.
They get very hoarse
In the winter, of course –
And a sore throat is no cause to laugh.

There once was a very old gnu,
Who was used by a chief in some stew.
He should have been told
The gnu was too old:
For stews, only new gnus will do.

The elephant never forgets:
Neither messages, shopping or debts.
He can take in his trunk
A whole load of junk —
And the small ones make fabulous pets!

There once was an oranguentingue
Who would eat nothing else but meringue.
He sat on the floor
And ate forty-four
Till the stupid old monkey went bingue.

It's easy to live with the djerbil:
His diet's exclusively herbal.
He just munches and crunches
Long vegetable lunches
And charms every ear with his burble.

A cheerful old bear at the Zoo
Could always find something to do.
When it bored him to go
On a walk to and fro
He reversed it and walked fro and to.

There was a young man who was bitten
By twenty-two cats and one kitten.
Cried he, 'It is clear
My end is quite near.
No matter! I'll die like a Briton!'

There once were three owls in a wood
Who always sang hymns when they could:
What the words were about
One could never make out,
But one felt it was doing them good.

There was a kind curate in Kew
Who kept a large cat in a pew:
There he taught it each week
A new letter of Greek –
But it never got further than Mu.

(No relation, one imagines, to the other curate from Kew
referred to earlier.)

If you meet with the Indian Rhinoceros
You might think he just looks preposterous.
But how would you like
A nose with a spike?
It would make even Ghandi ferocerous.

If there's one thing that Nature has taught us
It's the virtues of being a tortoise.
They can slumber, I hear,
More than half of the year
In the depths of their snug winter-quartoise.

You will find by the banks of the Nile
The haunts of the great crocodile.
He will welcome you in
With an innocent grin –
Which gives way to a satisfied smile.

A barber who lived in Belgravia,
Well known for his faultless behaviour,
Remarked to a baboon
Who came in his saloon
'Do sit down – but I'm damned if I'll shave yer.'

A cat in despondency sighed
And resolved to commit suicide.
She passed under the wheels
Of eight automobiles,
And after the ninth one she died.

There was a young girl called O'Brien
Who tried to teach hymns to a lion.
Of the lady, there's some
In the lions tum tum:
The rest twangs a harp up in Zion.

There was an old man from Khartoum
Who kept two tame sheep in his room.
'They remind me,' he said
'Of two friends that are dead.'
But he never would tell us of whom.

According to experts, the oyster
In its shell (or crustacean cloister)
May at anytime be
Either he or a she
Or both, if it should be its choister.

There was an old man of Dundee
Who molested an ape in a tree.
The result was quite horrid:
All arse and no forehead,
Three balls, and a purple goatee.

There was a young man named Colquhoun
Who kept, as a pet, a baboon.
His mother said, 'Cholmondely –
I don't think it's colmondeley
To feed your baboon with a spoon.'

There was an old spinster from Fife
Who had never been kissed in her life.
Along came a cat
And she said 'I'll kiss that!'
But the cat meowed 'Not on your life.'

There was a young farmer named Morse
Who fell madly in love with his horse.
Said his wife, 'You rapscallion
That horse is a stallion –
This constitutes grounds for divorce.'

The wife of a farmer in Stoke,
Always one for a dubious joke,
Caught his sow in the act –
And reported the fact
To her spouse as 'a pig in a poke'.

There was an old Scot named MacTavish
Who attempted a gibbon to ravish,
But the object of rape
Was the wrong sex of ape –
And the anthropoid ravished MacTavish.

There once was a blooming Great Auk –
Couldn't fly – and it hardly could walk.
The ignorant Picts
Used to beat it with sticks
For the pleasure of hearing it squawk.

It is the unfortunate habit
Of the rabbit to breed like a rabbit.
One can say without question
This leads to congestion
In the burrows that rabbits inhabit.

The Monster of Ness, with an 'Och!'
Green with envy, passed out in his loch,
Deprived of survival
By Anglesey rival
Llanfairpwllgwngyllgogogoch.*

*Experts in Welsh spelling may feel this well-
known place name has been rather curtly abbrevi-
ated by the demands of metre.

A Question of Degree

Universities have long been occasional factories of ribaldry, much of it in verse, but little recorded in Limerick form. Most British entries seem to come from Cambridge rather than Oxford, or Redbrick, perhaps because of the formidable difficulties of finding, for instance, two sound rhymes for colleges such as Balliol or Universities such as Sussex. Oriel has been celebrated, of course, and Wadham also has proved too hard to resist. As for the Fellow of Jesus recorded below, one can assume on internal evidence that Jesus College, Cambridge, is referred to.

On the other side of the Atlantic, research shows that Harvard has been recorded once, and Yale several times, most of them being unprintable. So, again, here follow some classics and some relatively unknown verses.

> There was a young student of Johns
> Who wanted to bugger the swans.
> But the loyal hall porter
> Said 'Sir, take my daughter –
> Those swans are reserved for the Dons.'

> These once was a student of Trinity
> Who ruined his sister's virginity.
> He buggered his brother,
> Had twins by his mother
> And then took a degree in Divinity.

The career of a Fellow called Castor
One day met with sudden disaster
When he came into Hall
Wearing nothing at all
And made a rude sign at the Master.

There was a young scholar of Kings
Whose mind dwelt on heavenly things:
His only desire
Was a boy in the choir
With an arse like a jelly on springs.

There once was a Master of Jesus
Who one night slept with two of his nieces.
To the first he gave twins,
To the second one quins,
And, to both of them, frightful diseases.

A complacent old Don of Divinity
Made boast of his daughter's virginity.
They must have been dawdlin,
The students of Magdalen –
It couldn't have happened at Trinity.

Nor, as one might expect, have the ladies been omitted –
at Cambridge, at least.

There was a young lady called Burton,
Who outraged the Fellows of Girton,
By cycling to town
Without wearing a gown
And, what's worse, without even a skirton.

The virtuous ladies of Newnham
Are preserved from the men who would ruin'em
By the tales that they've heard
Of the birds who have erred
And the morals the Fellows imbue in 'em.

From Oxford, also, there is a handful of classics:

There was a young student of Oriel
Who flouted all rulings proctorial.
He ran down the Corn
With a hell of a horn
And buggered the Martyr's memorial.

An effeminate Fellow of Lincoln
One night did some serious drinkoln,
Met a girl, now his wife,
Learned the true facts of life,
And blesses the day he got stinkoln.

There was an old Warden of Wadham
Who was secretly given to Sodom.
For a man might, he said,
Have a very poor head
But be a fine fellow at bottom.

As with rowing, this contest seems to give a clear lead to
Cambridge by seven to four. Two entries from Harvard
and Yale follow:

'Far dearer to me than my treasure,'
Miss Guggenheim said 'Is my leisure.
For then I can screw
The whole Harvard crew –
They're slow, but it lengthens the pleasure.'

There was a strange student from Yale
Who put himself outside the pale.
Said the Judge: 'Please refrain,
When passing through Maine,
From exposing yourself again in the train –
Or you'll just have to do it in jail.'

There once was a student of law
Who said, 'Legal wording's a bore.'
Amid raucous laughter
'Let us ban "Hereinafter" –
And "Whereas" and "Heretobefore." '

An amorous M.A.,
Said of Cupid, the C.D.,
From their prodigal use,
He is, I deduce,
The John Jacob A.H.

A maiden at college, called Breeze
Weighed down by B.A's and Litt D's,
Collapsed from the strain.
Alas, it was plain,
She was killing herself by degrees.

A Classical Master of Arts
Told his wife he was still keen on tarts.
Said she: 'That's just dandy,
To think you're still randy:
You still know your principal parts.'

There was a young lady of Eton
Whose figure had plenty of meat on.
She said, 'Wed me Jack,
And you'll find that my back
Is a nice place to warm your cold feet on.'

There was a young lady from Harrow
Who complained that her mouth was too narrow –
For times without number
She ate a cucumber
But she never could manage a marrow.

Out of the Universities, of course, have come a number of cleaner limericks which are ribald about serious and sober notions of various kinds, philosophical and scientific theories and personalities and phenomena.

There was a young lady named Bright
Whose speed was far faster than light.
She set off one day
In a relative way
And came back the previous night.

To this famous limerick, the author, Professor Reginald Buller, wrote a less well-known but equally illuminating sequel:

To her friends, that Miss Bright used to chatter:
'I have learned something new about matter:
My speed was so great
That it increased my weight –
Yet I failed to become any fatter.'

There was a young man who said 'Damn!
It occurs to me that I am
A creature that moves
In predestinate grooves:
Not a bus, nor a train, but a tram.'

Here are some lines on two more scientific phenomena –
the Fitzgerald contraction, and the Doppler effect:

A fencing instructor named Fisk
In duels was terribly brisk,
So fast was his action
The Fitzgerald contraction
Foreshortened his foil to a disc.

There was a strange fellow called Brecht
Whose penis was seldom erect.
When his wife heard him humming
She knew he was coming –
On account of the Doppler effect.

A scientist living at Staines
Is searching with infinite pains
For a new type of sound
Which he hopes, when it's found,
Will travel much faster than planes.

There was a faith healer from Deal
Who said 'Although pain isn't real
If I sit on a pin
And it punctures my skin
I dislike what I fancy I feel.'

There was an old man of Nepal –
Couldn't get Chomsky's wavelength at all:
While Teilhard du Chardin
Led him right up the jardin,
Levi-Strauss drove him straight up the wall.

Job's comforters now are emphatic
That his illnesses – whether rheumatic,
Sclerotic, arthritic,
Myopic, paralytic –
Were, quite simply, psycho-somatic.

There was a young girl of Shanghai
Who was so exceedingly shy,
That undressing at night
She turned out the light –
For fear of the All-Seeing Eye.

Here is Ronald Knox's famous advertisement, inserted in *The Times* classified, so tradition has it.

Evangelical vicar in want of a portable secondhand font would dispose of the same for a portrait (in frame) of the Bishop-Elect of Vermont.

Here too is versification of one of the Rev Sydney Smith's comments, which doubtless would have been put in limerick form originally had the style been properly developed during that witty cleric's lifetime.

Two fishwives from neighbouring premises
Perpetually courted their nemesis.
They could never agree
In their quarrels, you see,
For they argued from different premises.

There was a young student of Queens
Who haunted the public latrines.
He was heard in the john
Saying 'Bring me a don –
But spare me those dreary old Deans.'

Said Shakespeare, 'I fear you're mistaken
If you think that my plays are by Bacon.
I'm writing a book
Proving Bacon's a crook
And his style's an obscure and opaque 'un.

I don't like the family Stein.
There is Gert, there is Ep, there is Ein;
Gert's writings are punk,
Ep's statues are junk –
And no one can understand Ein.

As Bradley is said to have said,
'If I think that I'm lying in bed
With this girl that I feel,
And can touch, is it real –
Or just going on in my head?'

There was a professor called Dingle*
Who made physicists' nerve-endings tingle.
His travelling clocks
Caused grave mental blocks
In those who felt time should stay single.

* This limerick celebrates an interminable correspondence about
theoretical errors in Einstein's proposals on relativity, conducted in
various learned papers such as *The Times*, *Nature* and *The Listener*.

A Convocation of Curates

One of the many purposes of the limerick is to shock those who like to be shocked. Another is to deflate the pompous. For this reason religion is as handy a subject as sex (whether the fair sex or the unfair sex). Ribaldry is certainly best aired at the expense of dignity, and if that is true, then the church must continue to suffer in dignified silence. In the middle ages, the limerick would have been banned.

> These verses, one can but surmise
> Were not meant for clerical eyes.
> Should the Bishop and Dean
> Find out what they mean
> They ought to turn pink with surprise.

> And if, among Romish admirers,
> They stimulate naughty desires,
> Confess them, at least,
> To your neighbourhood priest,
> For the price of ten Ave Marias.

In theology, it is always thought correct to start at the top. Ronald Knox wrote this widely quoted verse about the philosophical theory that things only exist when someone is observing them:

There once was a man who said 'God
Must find it exceedingly odd
If he finds that this tree
Continues to be
When there's no one about in the Quad.'

Which produced an anonymous, but undoubtedly in-
spired reply:

Dear Sir, Your astonishment's odd
I am always about in the Quad;
And that's why this tree
Will continue to be
Since observed by Yours faithfully, God.

So much for the highest life. Of the lower ranks of the
Church, Bishops and Deans, on account of their rank,
and the variety of misdoings recorded, almost deserve a
section to themselves: although numerically, Vicars out-
number them quite comfortably.

There once was a Bishop of Bude
Who every so often got screwed.
He might have atoned
If he'd only got stoned:
But a Rev getting screwed – well, that's lewd.

There was a young lady of Chichester
Who made all the saints in their niches stir.
One morning at Matins
Her breasts in white satins
Made the Bishop of Chichester's britches stir.

The Bishop of Bath and Wells
Was wholly unconscious of smells.
Throughout the whole diocese,
No whiff was as high as his;
The odour of sanctity tells.

The unfortunate Dean of South Herts
Was caught importuning some tarts.
His good wife was shocked
When the Dean was unfrocked:
For the first time she saw all his parts.

A Dean who was rather a prude
Thus addressed a sunbather at Bude.
'Excuse me, but – er, Miss –
So much epidermis
Makes me feel that the cloth should intrude.'

Said the venerable Dean of St Paul's
'Concerning those cracks in the walls –
Do you think it would do
If we filled them with glue?'
The Bishop of Lincoln said 'Balls!'

There was a good Canon of Durham,
Who fished with a hook and a worm.
Said the Dean to the Bishop
'I've brought a big fish up –
But I fear we will have to interr'm.'

The Reverend Mr Uprightly
Was cuckolded daily and nightly.
He murmured 'Dear, dear!
I would fain interfere
If I knew how to do it politely.'

There once was a boring young Rev.
Who preached till it seemed he would Nev.
His hearers, en masse,
Got fatigue in the ass,
And prayed for relief of their neth.

There was a young lady called Tessa
A quite unrepentant transgressor;
When sent to the priest
The lewd little beast
Began to undress her confessor.

Many of the following encounters remind one of Sidney
Smith's sad remark 'The worst thing a Vicar can say is,
"I will see you in the vestry after service."'

There once was a curate from Kew
Who preached with his vestments askew.
A lady called Morgan
Caught sight of the organ
And promptly passed out in the pew.

There was a young lady of Tottenham,
Her manners – she'd wholly forgotten'em.
While at tea at the Vicar's
She took off her knickers
Explaining she felt much too hot in 'em.

There once was a Vicar of Horsham
Who always took every precaution:
Till one Ermyntrude
Let a stray sperm intrude –
And that was a case for abortion.

When a lisping young Curate from Merthyr
Asked a virtuous lady called Bertha
'Have you ever been kitht?'
She said curtly 'Dethitht!'
So he thought 'Well, she's false to me. Curthyr!'

An indolent Vicar of Bray
His roses allowed to decay.
His wife, more alert,
Bought a powerful squirt,
And said to her spouse: 'Let us spray.'

The robes of the Vicar of Cheltenham
Gave him pleasure whenever he knelt in 'em.
But they got rather hot
When he wore them a lot,
And the Vicar of Cheltenham smelt in 'em.

Our Vicar's an absolute duck –
But just now, he's down on his luck.
At the Sunday School treat
He tripped over his feet,
And all of us heard him say
'Now children, let us stand up and say Grace'.

A religious young lady from Berwick
Conceived a great love for a cleric.
But on finding this curate
Just wouldn't endure it,
Her passions grew truly Homeric.

A depraved young Parsee in Calcutta
Tried to write a rude word on a shutter.
He had got to CU
When a pious Hindu
Knocked him A over T in the gutter.

There was a young girl from Cape Finisterre
Who walked out each night with the Minister.
She said: 'I aspire
To a place in the choir' –
But some thought her motives more sinister.

There once was a Vicar of Clymping
Who earned tons of money from pimping.
When his Bishop asked why,
He replied with a sigh:
'Well, you can't have a man of God skimping.'

There once was a monk from Siberia
Whose manners were rather inferior.
He did to a nun
What he shouldn't have done
And now she's a Mother Superior.

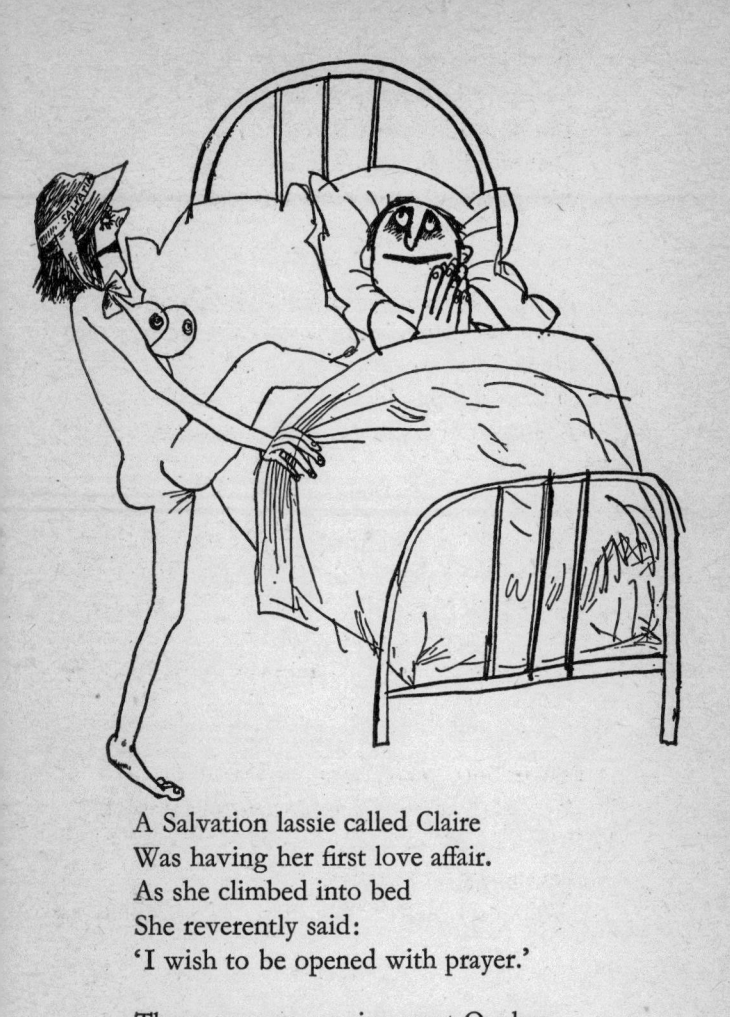

A Salvation lassie called Claire
Was having her first love affair.
As she climbed into bed
She reverently said:
'I wish to be opened with prayer.'

There once was an innocent Quaker
Who fell for a baker called Dacre.
Five minutes of lovin'
Put a bun in her oven,
And made the young baker forsake her.

There once was a pious young priest
Who lived almost wholly on yeast;
'For', he said 'It's plain
We must all rise again,
And I wanted to get started, at least.'

There once was a novice called Nell
Who, when going to Communion, fell.
She got up with a bound
Without looking round –
And said in a loud voice 'Oh hell!'

There was a young man of Belgravia
Who cared neither for God or his Saviour.
He walked down the Strand
With his balls in his hand
And was had for indecent behaviour.

There was a young girl with a feeling
That if she spent long enough kneeling
She'd feel the reception
Of the immaculate conception
(Note: the man under the bed came from Ealing.)

A bibulous Bishop of Norwich
Lived mainly on whiskey and porridge.
He liked to top up
His communion cup
With Pimms No.7 and borage.

Various Ladies (and Gentlemen)

The Limerick should certainly be an early target for the missiles of Women's Lib. Far too many girls are treated coarsely, and not enough boys. Historically, perhaps, that may be because women were treated both far too solemnly in the late nineteenth century (when the limerick first blossomed as an art) and far too dismissively – as sex objects: perhaps the twenty-first century will rectify the balance. Here, then, are large numbers of ladies who deserve to be preserved, and who have not so far appeared in earlier sections, and a few gentlemen as counterweights.

> There was a young lady called Valerie
> Who started to count every calorie.
> Said her boss in disgust,
> 'If you lose half your bust
> Then you're worth only half of your salary.'

> At shooting, Miss Myra MacLeod
> With exceptional gifts was endowed.
> But it wasn't her pistols
> So much as her Bristols
> That Myra's admirers admired.

'It's my custom' said dear Lady Norris
'To hitch rides from the drivers of lorries.
I see when they pee
Details hidden from me
At the wheel of my two-seater Morris.'

There was an old chap of Bengal
Who swore he had only one ball.
Then two little bitches
Pulled down his britches
And found that he had none at all.

There was a young hiker called Hilda
Who went for a hike on St Kilda.
They say that the climb
Is really sublime:
But it wasn't for Hilda – it killed her.

Did you hear of the musical bride
Who said to the groom at her side
'I never could quite
Believe till tonight
Our two instruments *would* coincide.'

There was a young lady named Mabel,
Who said 'I don't think that I'm able.
But I'm willing to try –
So where shall I lie:
On the bed, on the floor, or the table?'

There was a young lady called Myrtle
Whose features resembled a turtle –
The reason no lover
Did ever discover
If Myrtle the turtle was fertile.

There was a young lawyer called Rex
Who was sadly deficient in sex.
When had up for exposure
He said with composure:
'De minimis non curat lex.'

There was a young person called Herman
Who spoke both falsetto and German.
Behind the blond hair
There was *somebody* there
But its sex one could never determine.

'The beds are all full' said Miranda
To her beau, with commendable candour.
'And our antique chaise longue
Is not very strong –
So why don't we try the verandah?'

A wee Scottish lass called Miss Baird
Was seduced by the son of the laird
With some crude hanky panky
Above Killie Crankie:
She feared – but she dared, and she bared.

There was a young lady of Norwood
Whose ways were provokingly forward.
Said her mother, 'My dear
You wiggle, I fear
Your posterior just like a whorewood.'

There was a young lady called Kitchener
Who slipped on the quayside at Itchenor.
In spite of the pain,
She laughed like a drain
While the surgeon inserted a stitch in her.

There was a young fellow called Jones
Whose fiancée had prominent bones
And more than her share
Of superfluous hair
Around her erogenous zones.

There was a young lady called Maud
A sort of society fraud.
In the parlour 'tis told
She was distant and cold
But on the verandah, my Gawd!

There was a prim maiden called Campbell
Who got tangled one day in a bramble.
She cried 'Ouch, how it sticks –
But so many great pricks
Are not met every day on a ramble.'

There was a young fellow called Hunt
Who was punting his girl in a punt,
When she said: 'On the whole,
While you're wielding that pole –
I'd prefer you avoided my front.'

There was a young lady of Keighley
Whose principle charms in her teeth lay.
When they fell on her plate
She called out 'I hate
Mishaps of this kind, they are beathly.'

'Now really young man you're a bore,'
Said The Lady Priscilla Flax-Blore.
'I'm covered in sweat
And you haven't come yet –
And my God – it's a quarter past four!'*

There was a young lady called Brigid
Whose sex life was apt to be frigid.
So they used to begin
With a bottle of gin
Till the boy friend (not Brigid) was rigid.

An Argentine gaucho named Bruno
Once said: 'There is one thing I do know:
A woman is fine,
And a sheep is divine
But a llama is Numero Uno.'

* AM one assumes, rather than PM.

There was an old man of Madrid,
Who cast loving eyes on a kid.
Said he, 'Oh my joy,
I'll bugger that boy,
You see if I don't' – and he did.

There was a young lady named Smith
Whose virtue was mostly a myth.
She said: 'Try as I can
I can't find a man
Who it's fun to be virtuous with.'

A blonde woodwind player named June
Arrived at rehearsal too soon.
A man in the band
Put his flute in her hand,
And it changed to a contra bassoon.

There was a fair lady from Bangor
Who drove young men frantic with anger
By going to Matins
In see-through white satins,
Till the Vicar was forced to harangue her.

A buxom young typist named Baynes
At her work took particular pains.
She was good at dictations
And long explanations
But she ran more to bosom than brains.

A large-breasted lady from Cowes
Concealed a fat cat in her blouse.
Someone said 'I'll be blest!
Is *all* that your breast?'
And from her six tits came miaous.

There was a Señora from Alicante
Whose morals were notably scanty.
'I'm not at my best'
She said, 'Overdressed'
So she left off both brassière and panty.

An heiress from Abergavenny
Had offers of marriage full many.
She surveyed all the men
Very gravely, and then
Said 'Thanks, but I'm not having any.'

A flatulent plumber called Hart
Could not get his blow lamp to start.
So he then struck a match
Saying, 'Now it'll catch' –
Thus extinguishing Hart, lamp and fart.

On the chest of a barmaid in Sale
Was tattooed all the prices of ale.
And on her behind
For the sake of the blind
Was the same list of prices in Braille.

There was a young trollop from Trent
Who claimed not to know what they meant.
When men asked her age,
She'd reply in a rage,
'My age is the age of consent.'

A Gazetteer of Innocence and Infamy

Finding two good rhymes to a resonant, upstanding place name, such as Ladakh, not previously celebrated, is a great pleasure to the patient seeker of limericks. Unhappily it comes rarely. Most of the best towns (Crewe, Ealing, Dundee) have not only been immortalized before, but frequently.

None the less, patient research has produced almost a hundred entries for this light-hearted gazetteer. Almost half of these appear in print for the first time: and the rest are, in Miss Brodie's term, the crème de la crème. As Dorothy Parker is said to have remarked, 'If everyone at this party were laid end to end, I shouldn't be a bit surprised.'

> Said the affable King of Algiers
> To his fabulous harem 'My dears
> You may think it odd of me,
> But I've given up sodomy.
> From now on it's screwing.' (Loud cheers)

> A two-toothed old man of Arbroath
> Gave vent to a terrible oath.
> When one tooth chanced to ache
> By some ghastly mistake
> The dentist extracted them both.

There was a young girl from Australia
Who went to a dance as a dahlia.
When the petals uncurled
They revealed to the world
That the dress – as a dress – was a failure.

There was a young man from Belgrave
Who kept a dead whore in a cave.
He said 'I agree
That it's nasty of me –
But think of the money I save.'

There was a young man from Bengal
Who went to a fancy dress ball.
He went, just for fun,
Dressed up as a bun,
And a dog ate him up in the hall.

There was a young lady of Bude
Who walked down the High St quite nude
A policeman said 'What'm
Agnificent bottom' –
And smacked it as hard as he could.

She wore knickers of delicate mauve
And her temper was fiendish, or fauve:
She had a nineteen-inch waist,
And she married (in haste)
The Town Clerk of Brighton and Hove.

There was a young girl of Cape Cod
Who thought babies were fashioned by God.
But it wasn't the Almighty
Who lifted her nighty
But Roger the lodger, the sod!

There's a village called 'Come to the Good'
Where the people don't do as they should.
Every lad and his dad
Has gone to the bad –
And the women would too, if they could.

A hot-tempered girl of Caracas
Was wed to an ill-favoured jackass.
When he started to cheat her
With a dark señorita
She kicked him right in the maracas.

There was a young fellow from Clyde
Who once at a funeral was spied.
When asked who was dead,
He smilingly said
'I don't know – I just came for the ride.'

There was an old fellow of Cosham
Who took out his bollocks to wash'em.
But his wife said 'Now, Jack,
If you don't put them back
I'll jump on the damn things and squash 'em.'

Three bright little boys from the ballet
Had a lovely night out at the Palais.
But the end of their day
I am sorry to say
Was spent with three Burghers from Calais.

There was a young lady of Condover
Whose husband had ceased to be fond of her.
He could not forget
He had wooed a brunette
But peroxide had now made a blonde of her.

A handsome young gasman from Chester
Surprised a blonde housewife called Hester.
Said he: 'This is sweeter
Than reading your meter' –
So they then took a lengthy siesta.

A certain young gourmet from Crediton
Took some pate de foie gras and spread it on
A chocolate biscuit;
Then murmured: 'I'll risk it.'
His tomb bears the date that he said it on.

A lady while dining at Crewe
Once found a dead mouse in her stew.
Said the waiter: 'Don't shout
Or wave it about
Or the rest will be wanting one too.'

A railway official at Crewe
Met an engine one day that he knew.
Though he nodded and bowed,
The engine was proud
And it cut him – it cut him in two.

There was a young lady from Crewe
Who wanted to catch the 2.02
Said the porter: 'Don't worry
Or hurry or scurry
It's a minute or 2 2 2 2.'

There was an old fellow from Croydon
Whose cook was a cute little hoyden.
She would sit on his knees
While shelling the peas
Or pleasanter duties employed on.

There was an old lady of Chislehurst
Who before she could pee had to whistle first.
One day in June
She forgot the tune . . .
♪♩ – and her bladder burst!

There was a prim lady from Chiswick
Who consulted a Doctor of Physwick.
He tested her hormones
And sexual performones –
Then prescribed her a strong aphrodiswick.

There was a young lady from Devon
Who was raped in the garden by seven
Roman Catholic priests
The lascivious beasts –
Of such is the Kingdom of Heaven.

There was a young girl from Dundee
Who went down to the river to swim.
A man in a punt
Stuck an oar in her eye
And now she wears glasses, you see.

There was a young lady from Dorset
Who went to a pennyworth closet.
But when she got there
She could only puff air.
That wasn't a pennyworth, was it?

There once was a lady of Dover
Who said to her husband 'Move over –
I don't give a damn
For the charms of a man.
♪♩ . . . Come along Rover!'

There was a young lass from Dundee
Whose knowledge of French was 'Oui, Oui.'
When they asked 'Parlez-vous?'
She replied 'Same to you!'
A fine bit of fast repartee.

There was a young man from Devizes
Whose balls were of different sizes.
The one that was small
Was no use at all:
But the other won several prizes.

The conductor, with voice like a hatchet
Observed to a cellist from Datchet
'You have twixt your thighs,
My dear, a great prize –
An instrument noted for beauty and size –
And yet you just sit there and scratch it!'

There was a young girl from Darjeeling
Who could dance with such exquisite feeling
Not a murmur was heard,
Not a sound, not a word –
Save for fly buttons hitting the ceiling.

There was a young girl from Dumfries
Who said to her boy: 'If you please
It would give me great bliss
If, while fondling this,
You would pay some attention to these.'

There was a young lady from Erskine
Who had a remarkably fair skin.
When they said to her: 'Mabel,
You look nice in sable'
She replied: 'You should see me in bear skin.'

There was a young lady of Exeter
So pretty, the men craned their necks at her.
But some, more depraved,
Went further and waved
The distinguishing marks of their sex at her.

A knight in a chapel near Ealing,
Who had spent several centuries kneeling,
Said: 'Please keep off my arse
When you're rubbing my brass –
It gives me a very strange feeling.'

There was an old fellow from Fife
Who was garden mad all of his life.
He dreamt in his slumbers
Of giant cucumbers –
Which greatly embarrassed his wife.

A chap with a weakness for locks
Was making a tour of Fort Knox
When he spotted a fault
In the door of a vault
And abstracted a dozen gold blocks.

There was a young woman of Glasgow
Whose party proved quite a fiasco.
At 9.30 about
The lights all went out,
Through a lapse on the part of the Gas Co.

There was an old maid of Genoa
I blush when I think what I owa.
She's gone to her rest
And it's all for the best:
Otherwise I would borrow Samoa.

There was a young lady of Harwich
Who behaved very bad at her marrich.
She proceeded on skates
To the parish church gates
While her friends followed on in a carwich.

There was a young lady from Hadham
Very fond of the primitive Adam.
Whatever the name
Of the men on the game,
The madam from Hadham had had 'em.

There was an old barber from Hythe
Who shaved stubbly chins with a scythe.
He said: 'It comes cheaper
Than using a reaper,
Though it does make the customers writhe.'

There was a great lord in Japan
Whose name on a Tuesday began.
It carried through Sunday
Till twilight on Monday
And sounded like stones in a can.

A pansy who lived in Khartoum
Took a Lesbian up to his room
And they argued all night
As to who had the right
To do what, and with which, and to whom.

There was a young harlot from Kew
Who filled her inside up with glue.
She said with a grin,
'If they pay to get in
They'll pay to get out of it too.'

There was an old girl of Kilkenny,
Whose usual charge was a penny.
For half of that sum
You could fondle her bum:
A source of amusement to many.

There was a young farmer from Leyhill
Went to shit on the top of a high hill.
When his friends asked him: 'Was it
A pleasing deposit?'
He said: 'Vox et praeterea nihil.'

There was a young girl of La Plata
Who was widely renowned as a farter.
Her deafening reports
At the Argentine Sports
Made her much in demand as a starter.

There was a young plumber of Leigh
Who was plumbing his girl by the sea.
She said: 'Stop your plumbing,
There's somebody coming'
'I know', said the plumber, 'It's me.'

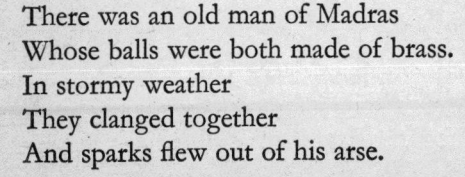

There was a young florist from Leeds
Who swallowed some packets of seeds.
In a month, stupid ass,
He was covered in grass,
And couldn't sit down for the weeds.

There was an old man of Madras
Whose balls were both made of brass.
In stormy weather
They clanged together
And sparks flew out of his arse.

There was a young girl from Madras
Who had a magnificent ass . . .
Not what you think,
Soft, round and pink;
It was grey, had long ears, and ate grass.

There was an old fellow from Malta
Who strangled his aunt with a halter.
He said: 'I won't bury her –
She'll do for my terrier.
She'll keep for a month if I salt her.'

A lecherous student from Leeds
One day had to pay for misdeeds.
When a man with a gun
Said: 'You'll marry her, son –
You must harvest when you sow the seeds.'

There was a young lady of Louth
Who returned from a trip to the South.
Her mother said: 'Nelly –
There's more in your belly
Than ever went in through your mouth.'

A policeman from Lewisham junction
Whose organ had long ceased to function
Deceived his poor wife
For the rest of her life
By intelligent use of his truncheon.

There was a young fellow of Lyme
Who lived with three wives at a time.
When asked: 'Why the third?'
He replied: 'One's absurd –
And bigamy, sir, is a crime.'

There was a young lady of Nantes
Who was très joli et piquante.
But her thing was so small,
It was no good at all
Except for la plume de ma tante.

There was a young girl of New Guinea
Who got very large neath her pinny.
She thought it was wind –
But found she had sinned –
And she had it removed for a guinea.

There was an old man from Nantucket
Who kept all his cash in a bucket.
His daughter, named Nan,
Ran away with a man,
And as for the bucket, Nantucket.

There was a young chap from Newcastle
Who could squash himself up like a pastle:
And in that position
Would give a rendition
Of God Save the Queen through his astle.

They bake some strange buns at Nuneaton,
With dough that's first whipped and then beaten.
They eat several tons
Of these fabulous buns,
But, south of Nuneaton, there's none eaten.

There was a young lady of Norway
Who hung by her heels in a doorway.
She said to her beau
'Just look at me, Joe,
I think I've discovered one more way.'

There was a young maid of Ostend
Who swore she'd hold out to the end:
But, alas, halfway over
From Calais to Dover
She done what she didn't intend.

There was a young man from Oporta
Who daily got shorter and shorter.
The reason, he said,
Was the hod on his head,
Which was filled with the heaviest mortar.

There was a young fellow from Ongar
Who had to be barred from the Congar.
The heat of the dance
Made his trousers advance,
As the congar got longar and longar.

There was a prim lady from Poole
Who dreamed she was chased by a bull.
The bawls were outsize –
And so were her cries –
It was all cock and bull, the young fool.

In Paris, some visitors go
To see what no person should know.
And then there are tourists
Who think they are purists
Who say it is quite comme il faut.

There was a young lady of Perth
Who was shy of her increasing girth
But, sadly, her figure
Got bigger and bigger
And BIGGER – till after the birth.

There was a young lady from Ryde
Who a sailor took on for a bride.
It wasn't the sailor
Who managed to nail her,
But the seamen inside her inside.

There was a crusader from Parma
Who lovingly fondled his charmer.
Said the maiden demure
'You'll excuse me, I'm sure –
But couldn't you take off your armour?'

There was a young lady from Reading
Who thought only plants were for bedding.
But she took to the pill,
And went swiftly downhill –
And nobody danced at *her* wedding.

There was a young lass of Pitlochry
Whose morals seemed truly a mockery –
When they found 'neath her bed
A lover instead
Of the usual item of crockery.

A glutton who came from the Rhine
Was asked at what hour he would dine.
He replied: 'At eleven
At three, five and seven,
And eight and a quarter to nine.'

A young violinist in Rio
Was seducing a lady called Cleo.
As she took down her panties
She said: 'No andantes –
I want this allegro con brio.'

There was a young girl from St Paul
Wore a newspaper dress to a ball:
But her dress caught on fire
And burned her entire
Front page, sporting section, and all.

Said a charming young lady of Padua,
'A peso? Why sir what a cadua!'
He said, lifting his hat,
'You aren't really worth that –
However, I'm glad to have hadua!'

A thrifty young fellow of Shoreham
Made some brown paper trousers and wore 'em.
He looked nice and neat
Till he bent in the street
To pick up a pin – then he tore 'em.

There was a young lady of Spain
Who took down her pants on a train.
There was a young porter
Saw more than he orter
And asked her to do it again.

There was a young lady of Stornaway
Who by walking, her shoes had all worn away.
She said: 'I won't mind
If only I find
That it's taken that terrible corn away.'

A tone deaf old lady from Tring
When somebody asked her to sing,
Replied: 'It is odd
But I cannot tell God
Save the Weasel from Pop goes the King.'

There was an old man of Tarentum
Who gnashed his false teeth till he bent 'em.
When they asked him the cost
Of what he had lost,
He replied: 'I can't say: I just rent 'em.'

There was an old man of Tashkent
Who slept with twelve goats in a tent.
When asked: 'Do they smell?'
He said: 'Oh, yes, quite well . . .
But so far they don't mind my scent.'

There was a young eunuch from Tonga
Who made up a dance called the Conga.
After dancing all day
He heard his Queen say
'I *do* wish your conga were longer.'

There was a young fellow from Tyne
Put his head on the South Eastern line;
But he died of ennui
For the 5.53
Didn't come till a quarter past nine.

When the civil engineer took advantage
Of a lovely young lady of Wantage,
The County Surveyor
Said: 'You'll have to pay her –
You've altered the line of her frontage.'

There was a strange man from Cape Wrath
Who bathed in some bright-coloured cloth.
When asked for the reason,
He said: 'It's the season –
It's not quite so hot as it wath.'

There was a dumb lady from York
Who at flesh to flesh contact would balk.
'Don't you think that you are
(Said she) going too far?
Why can't we just sit here and talk?'

There was a young weaver from Wapping
Who thought his first whisky was topping.
He swallowed it down
With a dubious frown
And hiccuped six weeks without stopping.

There was a young lady of Ypres
Who was shot through both cheeks by some snipers.
The tunes that she played
Through the holes that they made
Beat the Argyll and Sutherland Pipers.

There was a young lady of Havant
Who slept with an impotent savant.
Said she, 'Yes, we shouldn't' –
But it turned out he couldn't –
'So you can't say we have when we haven't.'

There are men in the village of Erith
Whom nobody seeth or heareth.
They spend hours afloat
In a flat-bottomed boat
Which nobody roweth or steereth.

All Human Life is There

Or so, proudly, used to claim *The News of the World* – that last refuge of teachers, parsons, scoutmasters and other deviationists. Some strange behaviour has been recorded in verse in many parts of this book: this last section includes a few further aberrations and comments on parts of the human scene unaccountably omitted from earlier sections.

> To an artist, a husband called Bicket
> Said: 'Turn your backside and I'll kick it.
> You have painted my wife
> In the nude to the life.
> Do you think for a moment that's cricket?'

> I sat next to the Duchess at tea:
> It was just as I feared it would be:
> Her rumblings abdominal
> Were truly phenomenal
> And everyone thought it was me!

Could this be the same Duchess as the heroine of our next?

The Duchess, when pouring out tea
Once asked: 'Do you fart when you pee?'
I replied, with some wit,
'Do you belch when you shit?'
And I think that was one up to me.

Connoisseurs of coition aver
That the best British girls never stir.
This condition in Persia
Is known as inertia:
It depends what response you prefer.

A lady with features cherubic
Was famed for her area pubic.
When they asked her its size
She replied in surprise
'Are you speaking of square feet or cubic?'

A remarkable race are the Persians
They have such peculiar diversions.
They make love all day
In the regular way
And save up the nights for perversions.

To his bride said the lynx-eyed detective:
'Can it be that my eyesight's defective?
Has your east tit the least bit
The best of the west tit?
Or is it a trick of perspective?'

There once was a maître d'hôtel
Who said: 'They can all go to hell!
They make love to my wife
And it ruins my life,
For the worst is, they do it so well!'

To his wife said Sir Hubert de Dawes:
'Fix this chastity belt round your drawers!'
But an amorous Celt
Found the key to the belt
While the Squire was away at the wars . . .

A dashing young dentist, called Hone
Attends all the nice ladies alone
And tries, from depravity,
To fill the wrong cavity –
Yet see how his practice has grown!

A Boy Scout was having his fill
Of a nice little Brownie near Rhyl.
'Yes, of course, I'm prepared,'
Said Patrol Leader Aird
'These girls are all taking the pill.'

The masses, declaimed Doctor Freud,
Are seldom so peacefully employed
As in the position
Described as coition –
So it's nice that it's widely enjoyed.

Some gels – and I don't understand 'em
Will strip off their clothing at random,
Without any qualms
To exhibit their charms:
In short – quod erat demonstrandum.

The enjoyment of sex (although great
For some years) is then said to abate.
It may well be so
But how should I know?
For I'm only seventy-eight.

Finally, a tribute to Norman Douglas. It seems that a
police doctor, an after-dinner speaker with a poor reper-
toire of jokes for such occasions, once borrowed Douglas' famous volume of limericks to ransack for a verse
which might enliven his speech at a police ball. The one
he picked was the famous:

There was a young fellow called Skinner
Who took a young girl to dinner.
At half past nine
They sat down to dine . . .
And by a quarter to ten it was in her.
(The dinner, not Skinner!)

In the event, fuddled by drink, he dropped his notes, and
attempted the limerick by memory, as follows:

There was a young fellow called Tupper
Who took a young girl out to supper.
At half past nine
They sat down to dine . . .
And by a quarter to ten it was up her . . . Not

Tupper . . .

Some bugger called . . . Skinner!

David Osborn

OPEN SEASON   **50p**

Clever, vicious and frightening – a novel to devour at a sitting . . .

Every autumn three seemingly respectable citizens set off on a hunting trip to the Northern Michigan woods.

Their quarry, a man and a girl . . .

Their object, rape and torture before they set their victims free to be tracked down and murdered.

This year the hunters find it's open season for revenge . . .

NOW A MAJOR FILM STARRING WILLIAM HOLDEN AND PETER FONDA.

Leslie Thomas

'A marvellously inventive and endearing writer with an undoubted gift for writing up comic and tender moments in and around bed' –
THE OBSERVER

THE VIRGIN SOLDIERS   30p
The virgin soldiers did not ask to be conscripted, they did not ask to fight. On the brink of war they all wanted to make one frantic attempt at living before dying . . .

'Truthfully tough, wildly sexy, hilariously funny, and as modern as tomorrow' – Carl Foreman

ONWARD VIRGIN SOLDIERS   45p
Bursting with life and bawdy humour, National Serviceman Brigg is now a regular army sergeant defending the Empire in the beds and bars of Hong Kong.

THE LOVE BEACH   30p
Preparations for a Royal visit to a South Sea island – a twilight colony ridden with petty jealousies, social taboos and love-affairs bring problems for everyone . . .

COME TO THE WAR   30p
Non-stop action amid the blankets and bullets of the not-so-virgin soldiers of Israel during the Six Day War . . .

These and other PAN Books are obtainable from all booksellers and newsagents. If you have any difficulty please send purchase price plus 7p postage to PO Box 11, Falmouth, Cornwall.
While every effort is made to keep prices low, it is sometimes necessary to increase prices at short notice. PAN Books reserve the right to show new retail prices on covers which may differ from those advertised in the text or elsewhere.